Bluebird

ISBN: 978-0-578-35732-4

Design & Layout by Rachel Clift
COVER ILLUSTRATION COPYRIGHT © 2022 BY RACHEL CLIFT

Bluebird

POETRY & PROSE

BY

Leah Esther Cordova

2022
POMONA
CALIFORNIA

THERE IS A BLUEBIRD IN MY HEART

THAT WANTS TO GET OUT...

- *CHARLES BUKOWSKI*

May this book reach the hearts of broken souls,
may these words ease your pain somehow
and offer you a sense of hope.
It does get better.
I promise it does.

May these words be a testament of a transformation and a metamorphosis. I am no longer the person who spilled these words many moons ago. In fact, I can no longer relate to her. I have since spread my wings. It is now my intention to release and let go, move on, and set free the chains that once imprisoned me and so, I write this book.

I write this book because I believe. I've grown. I have failed and learned. Because, I can help. Because I've survived the storm and because I am a bird with wings, meant to soar free, to be with love and in peace. Because I care. I care with all my heart. Because I have hope that we can heal and restore. Because I have faith in the goodness in people. Because I believe in myself. Because I believe in the great omnipotent being and source, because I want to praise the light that guides us all, and acknowledge the spirit that swims in our hearts. Because I have been blue. Because I've buried myself in a hole and considered it a tomb. Because I want to give with all my heart.

And so I write this book, after a long battle that I have fought with all my strength. I have been humbled and naked, restless and beaten, my wings have been clipped and my spirit imprisoned. Because I have shed heavy tears and because I have dragged my body on the dirt. Because I come from the pits of this world and because I've called onto God for rescue and I have been transformed. Because, I want to tell you, have hope and do not give up. This life is truly beautiful even if you are blue.

Dedicated to all the stars buried in the depths of the dark, in the pit of our society and hidden under the rug, I see you - shine through, keep shining through.

Leah Esther Cordova, 2021

Contents

CAGE

WINGS

CLOUDS AND BLUE SKIES

WHITE FEATHER

SONG

THE WHITE MARBLE CASTLE

CAGE

How would I begin to tell her story, her tale? How could I? From where? There are no words as there is usually none for such things, so I won't try. Instead, I'll document, in hopes that you may see what I see. She sits in a cage hung from a cloud in the skies. Her cage has a staircase, a series of black and white steps. She sits on the steps, on one side lies her pen and journal and on the other is her guitar. She is drinking a cup of coffee, thinking about birds, and how she always felt like one, always with a song in her heart.

I am like the caged bird
singing a monotone melody,
a tune of melancholy
awaiting to be freed.

I was born injured,
in a pit of despair.
Poverty ridden,
drug addictions,
abuse, betrayal, rejection -
all that was *normal*.
All that was real.
That is still *real* for millions.

Lonely is this place
in my chest -
hollow, echo, soundless.

My heart aches,
inside it is pouring rain.
There are no stars out tonight.
I've used up all their magic
and I've wasted all their shine.

Memories at times anchor one to the past
and while the past may have been beautiful, it is no way of living -
that is like clinging on to a ghost, a shadow, a shell,
that is no longer inhabited by anything living.
And I know this -
I know this all too well.

I know I am caging myself
but I have no code or key to set me free.

Bad idea to try to go meddling in the past
with the scent of old,
and memories that anchor and haunt.
It's like burying myself again
and I'm tired of digging myself out.

I can't tear off these ligaments
My heart might as well be caged in your ribs
To leave you?
I might as well cut off my limbs.

I am a mess, an utter mess -
stitched together merely by thread,
salvaged from the ravenous teeth of life
and graced to live it.

In my heart I have always felt a deep void
that could not wait to be filled.
It's when I sing, when I write, when I dance -
when I simply am that I feel fulfilled.
Even though I have always looked up at the gridded wired skies
with shoes hanging off telephone wires,
even though I heard helicopters breaking the wind,
sirens and screams of the city in the not too far distance,
even if I grew up behind a loud roaring freeway
and felt caged in wired fences,
I still heard the power of the rainstorm and thunder
breaking free even louder.
I'd still look up at the moon and felt that one day,
this dream, this promise, will one day blossom too.

Still blooming,
but barely alive.

I am bound by the reality
that we have to work to eat and eat to survive.
I am very aware of that annoyance and anchor
which binds us all from ever feeling free
If it weren't for this anchor,
who wouldn't I be?

I am all that I am
because of my struggles,
and I kiss those scars
and embrace them with love.

And all that I have suffered,
I've suffered alone.
And all that I have endured,
I've endured alone.
And no one can see my pain because I am composed but
I hush my demons and swallow them whole.

I have been a fool,
an injured fool,
like a moth with a broken wing.
I am faulty of many sins
and I have lost plenty.
I have nothing to boast about
and I have no pride left.
I live only now to tell you about it.

I've always felt a little strange,
somewhere else, nowhere really.
I am neither here nor there.
I have no identity.
I belong to nothing.
I don't even belong to me.

I have been used as an instrument
to ease the hearts of broken souls
But I lie far more broken
than any tiny screw or gear I have restored.

Rejection, the more you come around,
the more I get used to you being around.
I am not going to be afraid of you anymore
because I always come back stronger than before.

This is a lonely life - a solitary adventure.
With but few characters that enter and go.
Others who show you to other doors.
Others are lessons and others
who will never again return.

I spilled three droplets of tears on my sheet,
the rest have left a trail down my cheek.
When will the river run dry?
When will I ever cease to cry?

Can I just time travel to those old records of time?
when all was well and skies were blue,
and the roses grew?

The barbed wire fence
never stopped the rose from growing.

And sometimes, I bend the knee
to the negative voices in my head
I hear daily.

And when there is nothing to be said and done
that is when I most want to rage and beat, slit, cut
When matters can't change,
all I want to do is escape, escape, escape!
Let me out, let me rage
I'm angry, rabid, dangerous
and the demons inside are growing stronger by the minute.

CLOUDS
AND
BLUE SKIES

It is the late-afternoon sun, before it goes out into dusk, she lays there in her cage in the skies, staring at the waves and motions of the clouds. The clouds are so beautiful, the kind that are so elliptical, like a stone to a ripple. Each ripple soaks in all the rays of the sun and paints the sky with pastel ribbons. She lays there staring, contemplating -

Loved one, do not forget your roots.
They are your anchors that tie your step to your soil,
and your earth that loved you and raised you.
Loved one, your heart is born as a fruit of your soil,
And your blood is the honey of your fruit.
Loved one, your fruit is your word.
Your fruit is your voice
recognize it, and sing it -
lively bird!

Be courageous like the lion
and strong like the tree -
believe.

This is your life, your stage,
your film, your soundtrack,
and you are the main character.
Everything is possible,
even the impossible.

A good decision leads another
It doesn't matter when you start
It is as soon as you start.
All we have to remember is to start.

The truth is there is no perfect time -
it is now or never.

If you seem sure,
others will surely follow.

All is beastly and beautiful
and we are all beautiful demons.

Although we mean nothing
in the great expanse,
and are insignificant
in the ever-expanding galaxies
and milky-ways,
I am here
and you are listening.

To feel is beautiful
I wouldn't trade a song that strikes the soul for nothing,
even if it makes me sob.
If ever you feel blue,
know that you are not alone.
Everybody hurts.

Stop apologizing for being yourself.
Yes, you may be strange,
but we are all strange and beautiful.

And just think back and be proud
of all the progress you have made thus far.

We never know how good things are until it's past.
Sulk in every moment,
every kiss, smile or laugh
and hold on to it tight.
Life comes and goes in a flash.

One is surrounded by people who anchor or uplift,
always choose the latter.

We all deserve love.
Every single one of us,
and I will go on voicing it
until my last petal hangs
and my last breath,
released.

You have everything you need
to be all that you wish to be.
So be - be free, believe.
Your dream is this moment,
this instant, this second.
So paint this world with your palette.
Put something that has never been there before.
Put yourself out there, there is only one you in this world.

We need nothing else,
no one else.

We are a solitary universe,
a single star in the great expanse -
unique, miraculous and beautiful.

Love, be courageous and confident
because you have so much to give and be.
Give your time, give your hand.
You can - yes, you can.
You are unique and let them know.
Let the world know
and let the people see.
Be confident and courageous, my love.
Let be.

Beautiful, do not let your chains trap you.
Your chains blossom and your rags decorate.
They do not imprison rather they liberate.

Even a heart of gold can lose its shine if not kept.

Afterall, although easier said than done
we are more our habits than anything else.

The sky hooks my heart
like bait from a fisherman's rod.

So you had a good streak,
but sometimes the tides may be a little hard to overcome.
Now, look - even though your soul is about ready to burst,
and the cannons and bombs are about to explode, It's ok -
spread your wings, you can fly out of this cage.
Use your instrument, use your voice and sing,
your voice is your instrument-
use it.

I close my shutter eyes
to those who fog my window soul.

To those born like me,
born to the night,
born with the gray clouds hanging above,
have faith -
All we have to do is flip the whale on its belly.
Together we can.

My eyes feel like parachutes
and I am ready to wake up and dream

WINGS

Then she takes to the wind and spreads her wings to roam free, fly and dream. Her wings are her freedom, her peace, her solitude, where she is free to be all that she wishes to be. She is not always flying but when she is, her wings enable her to step in and out of her cage as she pleases. You see, for years she had been caged to her fears, anxieties and traumas but her wings have grown large, each feather collecting a series of dreams, hopes, passions and aspirations - anything that makes her light as a feather. Her wings are her sails, this way she can navigate the waves of the wind and the vortex of the clouds.

Music is my form of time travel.
I grow wings upon hearing a tune
and I am no longer blue.

Here or there, meaning all the same
We are where we *are*.

When my world collapsed I set sail,
and took to the wind aimlessly
I sat on cloud afer cloud
not realizing I have been falling incessantly

He brings joy in my heart
as if over-sized wings have grown on my back,
large enough to carry me.
I'm free alas!
And the wings on my back
Have grown twice my length-span.

I've perched on many clouds
thinking I was on cloud 9

I was right to love
I was wrong to love him

I've always believed in the one.
The one all the songs and novels have been written about
Life is more beautiful if we believe
Do you believe?
Doesn't a part of you want to believe?

I'll always leave the door open for you - always.
No matter the hurt, the pain, the heartache.
No matter if you are sick or ill.
No matter what you have done, who you have become -
20 years, 50 years, 100 years, a million years could pass us by
and I still have a place for you in my heart
and when I said forever I meant it.

I have loved and lost and I'd do all over again
If given a second chance.

To take an inch of love for an inch of pain
I will take any day,
any day at all.

"What do you want?" he asked,
"I want the impossible," she answered.

It's you. It's you.
It's always been you.
How can it be the end?
For you the rose bloomed
For you the sky moved it's hair of clouds from view
It's you. It's always been you.

For you I'll wait a lifetime
For you I'll be patient
For you I'll be loyal, babe
I'll be your confidant.

And the heat, the pull, the magnetic lure of
my heart was so drawn to yours.

Soulmates have the same hiding spots.

We shared an intimacy of spirit I've rarely seen
from the moments I first saw him, I fell so curiously.
I knew then as I know now, that it was written in the stars.

Wear your heart like the unhurt child within.

What I love... I love, I love so much
and yet to love, is one of the hardest things to do.

- Love is a verb.

Take it to my grave,
because there is no other truer thing than this:
All we need is love.

Yeah, I'm hurting for someone
but I am longing for something better.
Something I've wanted ever since I can remember.

Sadness is lovely
and to feel is beautiful.

If love was demonstrated
and this world could clothe our children with it,
poverty would rid itself and the wealth of our nation, restored.

- Love is everything.

If only I can yell it for all to hear
I wish for such courage
To face my fears
To fly away would be ideal
Surely there will be no tears

All I know is my heart,
and I've gambled it like a fool.

I'd very much like to escape.
Take off, spread my wings and sail the skies,
I'd like to dream with the stars
and extend my umbilical cords to the heavens above.

To love after you have been burned by the flame
is the hardest thing one can do.

I've always walked this life
with the compass of my heart pointing the direction
and I learned to speak the language of instinct and intuition.

Isn't it amazing how from one moment to the next,
you can be flying high as a kite
and then suddenly you find yourself deflated
and on the ground,
waiting to catch the next gust of wind?
Much like the sea, I can be as turbulent -
shifting and changing with my emotions.
I feel so deeply,
sometimes to a fault.

Even if I do not see a dime to my name
my dream will remain.

Aren't the most precious things small flashes,
too quick to grasp and too quick to describe?
They become a secret like the bluebird in my heart.

It is another beautiful day under the sun
and I am allowing myself to swim in the waters within.
The waters are calm and my streams braided with love.

Life can be so unexpected sometimes,
there is nothing and then suddenly
in a flash it passes by like a fast racing car
or a large wave you either ride it
or let it go by
and I want to ride this wave,
It's a big one I feel.

Since I've chosen to take this windy path,
It has been battle upon battle with no resolution in sight.
It's disheartening and at times, I wish I took the easy route.
But God knows, I've never been much of a sheep
and all my actions that have led me thus far
have come from a spring unknown to me
all I have ever done and all that I will continue to do
is to fulfill this calling within me.
I know you know what I mean -we all have this.
This tiny spark that if we allow it to ignite
we can make lightning grow out of the night
and I intend to ignite this burning passion inside.

I do believe that this is another door,
and I shall go as far as I can go.

Synchronicities are all around.
All we have to do is remove the block and walk.

I have lived very beautiful moments in my life, I forget all that I have lived.
I have seen the sun mist morning pastures of Honduras
in the early morning where I was woken up by the call of the rooster
and the morning song of the birds.
I spent hours upon hours laying on a hammock
singing my favorite songs and dabbling with the guitar.
I have fallen asleep to the moonlit night
in the wide open space, gazing at the mouth of the universe.
I have seen a wave the size of Moby-Dick himself,
threaten me with its omnipotence.
And when I went winding up the hills of Italy,
I wanted to kiss the foothills that have allowed me to behold its great beauty.
I have seen the sunset of New Mexico against its red-skin sand
bleed in a blanket of warmth.
I have many moments when I have been humbled like a grain of sand
and I had to swallow a lump of tears down my throat.
I have felt at times I've flown a car above the San Luis Obispo hills,
and I kid you not, it almost seemed like the California cows
were floating with the clouds.
My life has been so surreal, so lucid, and so spectacular.
I forget life is truly magical.
Books can be written about the characters I've met.
Should I tell you about the artist, the peacemakers and the romantics?
And I have met them all with a penny in my pocket and a pen full of dreams.
I have backpacked, couchsurfed, and volunteered.
I did work-exchanges, house sittings and writers residencies.
I have worked on farms, lived in a hostel, and lived in a car.
I have lived with the locals and eaten meals with them at the dinner table.
And I can go on and on and I intend to do more of this,
because to me this is what living is about.
The best adventures I've had was when I was penniless.

Gold, light, stars, bright,
honey, sun, moon -
all, in my spoon.

WHITE
FEATHER

Last night, she ventured into another world or portal in the sky, she has never navigated before but it is North, considering that she has been feeling light and airy with hope in her heart. There she was laying on a cloud and above her is a vintage blue truck flying above the bright blue skies full of white fluffy clouds, and attached to the bumper of the truck are kites, many kites, and people on unicycles and parachutes. Then, a hawk flies past her, and she turns her head over to see a row full of dandelions, blossoming and enveloping mound on top of mound. And looking at that whimsical sight she runs towards the row of dandelions and all of them lift up like feathers and twirl around her and just like that she wakes up.

I raise my voice to the heavens
Bring down your rope of hope
Bring down your ladder to climb
I want to dream
I want to fly.

I am the vessel with sails and you are the winds that steer
and let me not forget it that I am nobody
and what I have within everything.

I shall try to spend more time listening
Not to music composed by man
But the symphonies of the winds
and the song of God.

I am alone-
alone as if it were my first name
alone like the moon,
alone like the sea.
alone like the wind that swims past me
always alone
but I very much like being alone -
I feel whole,
I feel complete.

And again I turn to you, this pen-
because no matter how loyal a person can be,
all I have is myself.

I have to have faith in the universe,
because nothing is more beautiful
than when all is synchronized -
the winds, the ruffles of paper,
it is all so magical.

And here I am once again, I take to the pen-
To cleanse the palette of the mind
of chaotic brown mesh to a crystal clear zen
To comb and braid my tangled thoughts
To control the ebb and flow of the waves
crashing against the caves of my heart
For the most tranquil and pristine waters of peace and calm.

My adored people,
do not drown in your sorrows.
Hope floats - have hope,
rise to the edge of the pit and rescue your souls.
Do not be another body buried in the ground.
Do this and the sky will open a ladder to climb.

I have been on a whirlwind
to try to find the gold within
and let it spill it out
like honey from my lips

What if this pen is only my means of staying afloat,
just to keep my head above the water?
What if this pen is only meant to get me to the lifeboat
after being spit out of the belly of the whale?
What if I am meant to rise on my feet and walk on the shore?
What if I am meant to raise my wings and soar?
What if this pen is only guiding my path to a new land
I have been afraid to explore?
I surrender to this pen and the shore,
it knows best and I'll go wherever is better than before.

Writing, you ask? It saves me.
It is the torch that lights a dark desolate path.
It is my lifeboat from a sea of emotion.
It is my last gasp of breath.
The last glimmer of hope.
The last flame of warmth.
This pen has saved me.
And if it weren't for this pen,
I'd surely be dead.

I'd drink to forget,
I'd play guitar to console me,
I'd smoke pot to numb me,
I'd write to keep me from drowning
Otherwise, I'd surely be dead.

All I care to offer is a remedy for the lost dark souls.
So, I have to remember that this fight is not my own
but ours and I shall shatter my ego and rid myself of my image.
I don't know what or who or how -
all I know is that I intend to let go
and let the inner pure thing thriving to breathe flow.
And may it be, and may it be so.

And there will be many
who claim to be alongside you and then betray.
Everyone can potentially stab your soul with a blade.
But you are the only thing I have,
 you - this spirit within,
that I am learning to adore more than anything.
This pen, this voice, this ink will never betray.

Always dedicate time to your pen.
Remember the stride of ink gliding through the sheet.
Remember your voice dying to break free.
Set it free - dance, sing, write, release.
Tell them what you know.
Give a hand and share your heart to this world.
Speak to your lost brother and your heartbroken sister.
Speak to the broken children and your hopeless friends.
Speak to the homeless, the incarcerated, the slaves.
Speak to them all who need a piece of the gold within.

SONG

She owns a lantern to guide her in the dark and when she is in doubt. It is a beautiful mosaic lantern with colors of pastel green, pink and lavender purple, the same as a sunset at dusk with the array of pastel colors in the skies. This is no ordinary lantern, when lost, and in need of some guidance she uses it to guide her through an unknown avenue in the undiscovered, unmapped skies. She confides in it, and has faith in its light.

I'm just another soul looking for her place in the world
an outcast looking for her home
an artist floating like a kite in the skies
another person looking for her own peace of mind.

I am no mystery -
Just a shy girl,
plain as can be.
I wear my emotions,
transparently.

Never again, will I apologize for my dialect
or the color of my skin.
The Southwest is my land and from this soil I was raised
And the color of the sand is the color of my flesh.

Names and dates fail me,
instead ask me how it felt and what it meant.

No, not me.
I will not be swept away.
My roots are buried deep and I am too strong
I've been through too much to give up.

It may be that the blood in my veins
carry both a blessing and a curse.
My mother and my mother before her
have all carried in their eyes
the sad glare of deep emotional pain
but a voice of velvet soft grace
and a touch of a rose petal kiss.

I feel, I feel too damn much-
that is both a blessing and a curse.

I've been rejected from my own country
and I a foreigner in my mother's land,
I am from nowhere,
but also, I am from everywhere.

I know I'm peculiar.
I'm beautiful in a dark, moth-like way.
I am not beautiful to most,
still - I deserve to be desired.
I deserve love.

Anything worth doing
is worth doing fully invested,
with all my energy.
I need to make way,
I need to break away.

I adore that moon
as if my heart were tied to it
by an umbilical cord.

Who am I not to let go, let be, be bold?
Who am I to hinder that creation?
Who am I to go against it?
Who am I to question it?

I wish to be a better person
to be a role model
a person who loves life
and a person who uses her talents
for the betterment.

Maybe I was a bird in a past life-
a hawk, an eagle, an owl
Otherwise why else would I have this song in my heart?
I don't know why,
but I have to trust it.

My voice is my instrument.
It would be foolish of me to waste it.
Even if it means failing.
I know how to lose.
I've lost so much already.
So, I'd rather lose to something I am passionate about
than to lose to something I don't care for.
This life is to be lived - to enjoy.
And how they say, "tenemos que chupar el jugo del dia"
or "we need to suck the juice of the day,"
like the honeybee or the hummingbird.
So, let's do it. Let's be happy.
Here is to happiness and to our pursuits!

I am not such a mother to nurture the word
and mimic the rose that grew
from the womb of this earth.
I am not such a mother to bury my seed in this sheet
as I am am only a seed, a stone, a ripple of the word
and I can only hum its great song.

Do not forget about your people, my love.
The humble people. The poor people.
The beaten, the forgotten, the invisible -
that is the seed you were born from
and the root that has raised your voice from the depths.
Do not lose your love for your people,
your land, your soil, your earth.
Do not forget your mother tongue -
there lies your spirit and breath.

I am doing my part in leaving my mark—
my ripple for a cause.
This is my part.

I am nothing and I come from nothing
So I have nothing to lose
and everything to gain.

I'd rather rejoice in the gold in our people
even if it is a small nugget in the seas
and relate in all that binds us as one
rather than our polarities.
I'd rather look into your eyes with love
and I'd rather find truth than contradiction.
I'd gladly shake hands with you all,
because we are more similar than different.

THE
WHITE MARBLE
CASTLE

And so, she carries on keeping the flame within, the spark in her heart alive. This tiny spark that if she allows it to ignite can make lighting grow out of the night and turn her world into a bright kingdom. She's had dreams about this kingdom and the white marble castle.

This white marble castle rests in the mountain tops of only God knows where. Her wings have taken her there only a couple times. In order to reach it she has to walk through a green forest of tall ancient trees. Once she is close enough the first thing she sees are the white gates. They are simple gates, gating gravestones and a beautiful fountain at the center. A grand and miraculous fountain, made out of white marble with intricate designs and artistry. And there in the far distance lies the white marble castle.

It looks like a monochromatic photograph of white hues, light grays, white mist. It feels bright and airy. There is almost always a light fog each time she has been there. Upon entry, lies a white marble staircase resting in between two large white marble pillars. And on top of the staircase lies an empty throne. She walks towards it with confidence and she can even hear the echoes of her heels on the marble floor approaching her great right to her throne.